Wet Welded Together

Louise Grassi Whitney

Wet Welded Together

Collected Poems

by

Louise Grassi Whitney

Many Names Press
Capitola/Santa Cruz County
California USA

First Edition.
ISBN 10: 0-9773070-4-2
ISBN 13: 978-0-9773070-4-3
Library of Congress Control Number: 2012948559

To order direct: Kate Hitt 831-427-8805
                     khitt@manynamespress.com
                     ManyNamesPress.com
                     P.O. Box 1038, Capitola, CA 95010

                 Louise Grassi Whitney 707-299-9330

Printed in USA with archival & environmentally sound paper by BookMobile.

Distributed by ItascaBooks, wholesalers to the trade 800-901-3480.

Grateful appreciation is given to the editors of the publications in which these
poems first appeared: *Sandhill Review* ("Winter in Hamlin", "Beach Shoes")
*Bellowing Ark, Caesura, Medicinal Purposes, Mudfish, Poets On, Rhino,
Sojourner, Habersham Review, Black River Review, Atlanta Review* and the
Marin Poetry Center *Anthology 2012* (horse themed)

Louise G. Whitney was nominated for a Pushcart Prize when *Dominatrix* was
first published in *Disquieting Muses*
(http://www.dmqreview.com/nov00/whitney.html).
Many of these poems appeared earlier in chapbook form: *How Odd, Wet Welded
Together, Xmas 1992, Communion, Suzie Sits Down Laughing, Semiformal.*

Images of 30,000 year old cave paintings of the horse, bison, tiger, mammoth and
rhino by early Upper Paleolithic homo sapiens from public domain on Wikipedia
and donsmaps.com. "Woolly Mammoth" in the Royal British Columbia
Museum, Canada, photographed by Gerald Legere, used with permission.

In Memoriam

Portrait of my father
before my birth
longing to meet him

Acknowledgments

I would like to thank my spouse, Dr. Karen Lee Smith for all her loving support—and wish there was another word to describe our wonderful relationship. I would like to thank my youngest son and muse, Eli Whitney. Grateful appreciation goes to my friends Victoria Shorr and John Perkins for inspiring me with their book-making expertise, and to Clea Koré and David Fairchild for their loving care. Special thanks to my superb publisher, Kate Hitt, without whom we would have nothing.

Mount Shasta

CONTENTS

One: Revenge on Venice

The Explorers Club 1

How Odd 2

Confess 3

If My Father Were Here 4

Ashes 5

Regret 7

Divorcée 8

Another Failed Creek Crossing
with My Egyptian Mare 10

Witnesses to my Disgrace Are Being Removed 11

Remember This 12

Stigma 13

Blessings 14

Following Her 15

Song of Burag 16

How Patience Lost Her Religion in Las Vegas 17

Shelly's Sister the Slut 18

Revenge On Venice 19

Two: Asylum

Tuesday Morning 23

Code Words 24

The Reliable Body 25

Entitlement 26

Marco | Polo 27

Rear View Mirror 28

29   Eli and Louise's Retardation
30   Mom, Tonapah Was the Greatest Horse
      in the World, Wasn't He?
32   On Finally Becoming a Good Mother
33   Beautiful Eyes
34   The Miracle of Eli and the Floating Stone
36   Sultans of Discombobulation
37   In That Case
38   The Secret Sorrow of Drooling Cats
39   Eli's Hyena
41   Asylum
42   Promises of the Wild
43   The Secret of Poetry
44   Recollection at Fourteen (A Boy's Turbulent Days)

Three: No Coin, No Ferry, No Oars

47   About the Author at Fifty
48   Plate Tectonics
49   Small Snail Meditation
50   No Coin, No Ferry, No Oars
51   Under Oak
52   Dominatrix
54   The Blade that Spares None
55   Butterfly Garden

CONTENTS, Continued

Queen Elizabeth the First 56
The Hotel Think About It 57
What We Learned at the Blue Bird School 58
Oh My God It's Hector 59
Mellifluous 60
Rondonia, Brazil 61
Thunder Road Home 62
Muse of the Seraglio 64
Hildegard von Bingen at
The Blue Mermaid Motel 65
Narrowing the Possibilities of Life Between Us 66
Forkéd Tongue Incantation 67

Four: Woodstock

A Valentine 71
Slow Lava 72
It Hurts to be Alive 73
What the Thunder Said 74
Belladonna 75
Log Book 76
Moon Mood 77
Music 78
Nitrous Oxide 79
Sargasso Sea 80
Following the Place at the Tip of My Tongue 81
Armor 82
And to My Granddaughter, Emily Hope Whitney,
I Leave My Diamond 83

84   Thoroughbred
85   Chantress of Amon
87   Conference of the Mute
88   Optimism of Crows
89   Address Book
90   The State
91   The Silence of Knives
92   Woodstock

Five: The African Queen's Tea Party

95   Canada Goose
97   Summer Reading in the Hamptons
98   Learning to Listen
99   Arsenic is Made With Peach Pits
100 Preparing her Orgasmic Memory
101 Winter in Hamlin
102 The Woman Who Fed Animals
103 Digging to China
104 An American Story
105 Labyrinth
106 Horse Power
107 The African Queen's Tea Party
109 Receiving the Fiftieth Rejection Slip
     After a Run of Beginner's Luck
110 Wet Welded Together
111 Beach Shoes
112 Dust Ruffle

Part 1:

Revenge on Venice

The Explorers Club

Take, eat; this is my Body, which is given for you.
Do this in remembrance of me.

At this point in Holy Communion,
she would picture the frozen prospector
on the slopes of Mt. McKinley,

from whose thigh her beloved grandfather
had carefully carved a steak.
After photographing the ravished thigh,
he cooked the steak with onions

and ate it.
Not because he was hungry,
but because he could.

Family lore celebrated this cannibalism,
hand colored the photographic plates
of the prospector and his diminished thigh
kept them in a drawer next to the sofa.

When she turned ten, steaks
from a mammoth, frozen in Siberia,
were flown to a unique dinner at the Explorers Club.

She and her grandfather feasted on the extinct,
not because they were hungry.

As a young woman in Manhattan,
she never did indulge in cannibalism,
but a ravishing woman offered her soul and body.

She took this delicious offering
because she was hungry
and because she could.

How Odd

My father's sacred crow call
lived on the upper shelf in the downstairs
closet above the winter coats.

The crow call always started
the ritual of pulling the stuffed owl,
shotgun and jacket with huge pockets

out of the downstairs closet
into the cut corn fields of fall.
He called it *crow shooting*

and took me, his first born, when
I finally turned six. I crouched
behind his bulwark back at the edge

of the red woods. He called across
the corn to the crows flying,
enchanting them toward us.

He fired twice. Two black bodies dropped
from the sky. He broke the barrel,
ejected the spent shells

still smoking, they struck my chest
gently and I dropped to the ground,
the incense of gunpowder proof

that I was killed. I plainly heard
my father chanting, *The shells are spent.*
You are not dead, not dead.

Nonetheless, I was. How odd
that heaven was so familiar
as he cradled my limp body home.

Confess

Confess you're willing to forget
that each and every day,
all the water of the Chesapeake Bay
was filtered—no, purified,
by endless beds of oysters.

So many oysters
that you passed a law
against feeding them to slaves
more than three times a week,
lest they sicken from a surfeit of smooth meat.

Are you too numb to remember
wading, long ago, chest deep,
when you could clearly see your toes?

Today, if you swim underwater
in the Bay of Tears, you can open
your brackish eyes wide without pain
but can't see the hand in front of your face.

If My Father Were Here

My son Eli can't speak
but he loves french fries

and I love him above all. Sweet Eli,
born to teach patience and acceptance

except today at McDonald's,
where he reaches over to the next table

with his long elegant arm
to grab a handful of a fat man's potatoes.

The man snarls, "Get that retard out of my food."
I strike, a fistful of patrimonial rage:

"If my Father were here
 he would kill you."

Ashes

I used to want my ashes scattered
on the gentle hill behind my house in California,
just where you enter the oak forest
after the first canter of the morning.

Not the steep hill facing west
covered with gray-green sage.
Too alien, not good for ashes.
No, that place must face east
toward my childhood

in the rolling hills of Maryland
where I rode with Old Joe the groom,
born a slave.

He'd sing me his song,
I've Got Hounds of My Own...
his dialect so thick,
I never really understood much
of what he said or sang,
but I never for an instant forgot
he was born a slave.

He was a tiny magic man who disappeared
into the inner city of Baltimore
on his horse
and reappeared in the country each day
always riding, always believing in horses.

One fall, Old Joe's saddle slipped
while we cantered through the woods,

and I thought I was looking at his death
as he fell, dropping his harmonica.
He wasn't hurt, but his old eyes
couldn't see little things.

I became his eyes,
looking for the harmonica
on my hands and knees
in the red and yellow leaves,
Old Joe holding the horses
like he did as a slave.

A perfect place for ashes.

Regret

We rolled our youth in joints
papered with toy money, complete
with serial numbers.
My brilliant brother
dialed these numbers on a dare
and got the White House.

This morning my brother, now rolling
in real money, calls for
our tri-annual talk.
Our mother is doing well
with her cancer, while our father
is getting slower. Our cousin
is trying to change the date
of the family reunion.

I am dying to tell my brother
that Gabriel the angelfish
miraculously recovered last night,
but I don't.

Divorcée

Fill large kettle 3/4 full of water
Bring it to a rapid boil
Add 2 tablespoons salt
For each quart of water

Drop in:
    1 live wife
    1 live husband
    Grasp just behind the neck

After dropping each in,
Let the water boil again

Lower the heat

Hire the lawyer.

Cover the kettle and simmer:
    2 years for long marriages
        with 3 or more children,
    1 year for shorter marriages
        with children,
    6 months for marriages without children.

Allow to cool in the broth or
if people are to be served hot
lift from the broth and drain.

To shell a cooked divorcée
and remove the meat:

Place the divorcée on her back

Twist off her rings and pretensions
Separate her soul from her body
Break off her ties with her in-laws.

Stick a fork into the
          bone of her tail and
Push the meat out in one piece
Remove and discard her
          old class status
Substitute a much lower one

Garnish with parsley
and melted butter.

Serve up to the work force
on chipped plates.

Another Failed Creek Crossing with My Egyptian Mare

The third time you refuse
to cross the creek
I use the whip,
defiant of your royal Egyptian blood.

Between my knees you broadcast
bridled hysteria,
not with piercing screams
and high hoofed pawings,
but with shivering micro sidesteps
and wildly questioning ears.

Suddenly I hear the roar of the Red Sea.
I can see, I can feel Pharaoh's horses,
desperate noses thrust above the water,
drowning as the sea closes,
Moses triumphant on the far shore.

Is this ancient failed crossing
imprinted on every cell of your body?

Witnesses to my Disgrace Are Being Removed

All these deaths make me happy.
Soon there will be no one to remember
those disarrayed nights

sleeping on the backs of sharks,
monsters of the deep, baited with fetid
bowels and the severed heads of horses,

hammerheads with galactic eyes,
hooked, spiked over the gunwales,
sardined in the bilge, twitching.

The world is growing lighter.

Remember This

When the nuns warn you
about the lies of a love-making man,

remember
that the mind of man
is less tortuous when making love
than when he speaks of armies and governments,
utters strange and dangerous nonsense
to please the bats at the back of his soul.

in love-making
you can meet him
with lies of equal force.

For a female governed,
there are few repartees
she can make
to the man who governs.

Stigma

Being different in kind
rather than degree,
I have always made people nervous,
wielding marriage and motherhood like broadswords,

the birth of my third and last child
finally disarmed me.
No amount of kissing, singing,
or feigning erotic interest in men

could coax this baby
to pick up his head, roll over or crawl.
Stigmas psychotically circled my home,
wings beating at the windows,

shattering as they burst in.
They sank razor talons into my back
bent over my strange baby's crib.
I would never pass again.

Blessings

When I was thirteen Bishop Moore
laid his hand on my head where
I ecstatically received the apostolic
blessing that went in a direct line
back to the hand of Jesus.

I silently swore to give up lying
and live a pure life as befits
one so privileged to be touched
one thousand nine hundred and fifty-seven
years after the fact.

At the celebratory lunch
to honor my passage to perfection,
I lied three times.

I don't remember the lies, but
I do remember
my sorrowful realization
that lying is obligatory
if you seek blessings from
Bishop Moore.

Following Her

Even in Venice

she travels with her herd of high-strung horses
stowed in a laden gondola, gliding
into the landing of the Palazzo Grassi.

Following her, the horses jump onto the platform
one by one: Tonapah, Bezatella, Nefeserra, Hypatia.
So many she can't remember all the names.

Childhood ponies from Maryland, highsteppers
from New York, trail horses from California hills
all stream into the great hall of the Palazzo,

thundering round the marble columns
after their cooped up voyage from America.
Lathered and trumpeting, they storm the grand staircase,

pass life-size frescoes of masked Venetians at ease,
hooves ringing on smooth mosaic floors,
confused by ceilings full of Neptune's naked women
riding fish-tailed horses from the lagoon.

Song of Burag

I am the refuge and rhythm of emptiness.
Like the desert-bred creeds of the prophets,
I come to you across sands
strewn with broken faiths.
        No mercy for failure

Sleek and slender, I can thrive on locusts.
Seven days without water,
I will answer the call to battle
without first quenching my thirst.
        No sympathy for weakness

My ancient lineage is sung by the poets.
It is written in the Koran:
For every barley-corn fed to me,
Allah will pardon: one sin.
        No mercy for failure

I will carry you to heaven
for I am the wind made flesh,
Burag,
lead mare of the prophet Mohammed.

How Patience Lost Her Religion in Las Vegas

A bedraggled rich girl
from a founding Las Vegas family

is daily dispatched to the nuns,
hungry.

Her boozed up mother, dimly aware
that mothers provide bag lunch,

instead makes
a year's worth of olive sandwiches,

freezer-burned from poor wrapping.
The nuns impressed with the girl's heritage,

are only vaguely concerned with her dirty scrawn.
They ask occasionally if she has eaten breakfast.

"Oh yes—my mother made me crêpes suzette,
drew me a deep bath, dried me with fluffy towels,

laid out fresh clothes, brushed my hair
with the softest touch. . . ."

"Ah, Patience," murmur the nuns,
"Surely you are blessed."

Shelly's Sister the Slut

Shelly's sister the slut
uses words like fiduciary
this and fiduciary that.

She wears business suits with low-cut
blouses and skirts slit up the leg.
Shelly's sister the slut

steals other women's husbands, fucks
them over financially
with fiduciary this and fiduciary that.

From their pockets or their pants, she sucks
up money and language.
Shelly's sister the slut

steals other people's wives, fucks
them with her fingers full
of fiduciary this and that.

She has never had much luck
with happiness.
Shelly's sister the slut
is confused by this. And that.

Revenge On Venice

*The Capgras Delusion: A lost sense of familiarity with something
or someone encountered before. The opposite of déjà vu.*
—The Harvard Mental Health Letter, February 1999

An exotic breed of lagoon animal
has left behind a seashell
pink, convoluted,
a bewitching inheritance
I hoped to claim.

I was deluded,
imagined myself more than a tourist,
a daughter of Venice
returning to my palazzo on the Grand Canal.
But it's a museum now,
my branch of the family, American.
So I paid my lira and gawked like the others.
What did I expect—
La Signora Grassi to walk out of the eighteenth century,
down the grand staircase, and invite me
into her gondola to glide to Piazza San Marco
for a hot chocolate?

I'll show Venice who I really am,
no lagoon animal here.
I'll shrink this town to the size of a grapefruit,
securing all statues of goddesses, winged lions
to the plank platform on which the city rests.
I'll untie all gondolas from their moorings,
cover the city with a watertight dome

blown by Venetian glass makers.
I'll fill the dome almost to the top with salt water,
then seal it.

When I turn it over with one swift motion
gondolas will bob to the surface.
The weight of the city will pull the pilings out of the ooze
until the whole city perches on the points
of her highest campaniles.

I'll expose Venice's foul pilings
until they stick straight up,
a slimy forest of denuded oak.

Part 2:
Asylum

Tuesday Morning

Escape from necessity? Like children? But one would lose the value of life. —Simone Weil, "First and Last Notebooks"

I struggle with the broken shade
in my bedroom. I do it every morning—
to shed light on the day, the spring.

I put away the eternal dishes
in the kitchen. I always do—
to clear a path for Tuesday morning.

I call, make plans for my youngest son
to come home for the weekend. I do every Tuesday,
trying to ignore the monumental fact
that he has never spoken a word.

I buy diapers for him, struggling not to dwell
on the adolescent mustache on his sweet upper lip,
or the inescapable fact that I will buy diapers
on Tuesdays until I die.

Code Words

A powerful American tribe,
white, under siege,
calls to each other softly
inherited words of privilege,
comforting code words of belonging.
  Curtains, not drapes
  Ice box, not refrigerator
  Rich, not wealthy
  Place, not property
  House, not home
  Help, not servants
  The office, not work
  Juif, not Jewish
  Silly, not shallow
  Foxhounds, not dogs
  Dinner coat, not tuxedo
  Stockings, not hose
  Beau, not boyfriend
  Having a baby, not pregnant
  Sofa, not couch
  Tomaato, not tomato
  My onnaise, not may onnaise
  Picture, not painting
  Princeton or Harvard, not college
  Fat, not heavy
  Fairy, not homosexual
  Pocketbook, not purse
  School, not high school
  Attractive, someone you are drawn to,
          not necessarily good looking
  Amusing, not slightly appalling.

The Reliable Body

I want to marry your husband.

The wife, stunned, stared at the wine
bottle between them until it glowed
so intensely that she switched her attention
to the wood grain of the table,
wondering what wood it was
and if anyone had fed the horses.

Her reliable body stood up
to check itself out.
Hair, needs a cut
Mouth, big smile
Shoulders square, relaxed
Hands on hips
Legs steady on the tile floor

Start again
Hair needs a cut
Mouth, big smile
Shoulders square, relaxed
Lucky the children are in bed
Hands on hips
I could throw her out
Legs steady on the tile floor

Start again
Hair needs a cut
Mouth, big smile. . .

It's over, you can have him.

Entitlement

So what did Dad do with all the money?
Why isn't there anything left for us?
they hiss at the windshield.

Moods surge off the wide backs of my sons
as I fiddle with heat control,
blowers and wipers, and we suffer

through the storm in my shrunken Volkswagen.
One son laments a credit card debt
amassed in college to save face.

Now he is a teacher on the treadmill
some rich relative should
stop.

They blame an irresponsible father
for pulling the silk rug
from under their expensive shoes.

They feel themselves fading,
fading in a fogged-up car, belittled
by a winter storm that would vanish

if only
they had the money they deserve.

Marco | Polo

Privileged Americans know a secret mantra
for opening commercial markets in China.
When very young, the hopeful commercial heroes-to-be
must chant the magic words: *Marco Polo*

a thousand times, in a clear voice
around a swimming pool. To find a player
in the water, you close your eyes and chant, *Marco*
to friends who must chant back, *Polo.*

Thus the spirit of Marco Polo enters
the young bodies at cellular level. Later,
marketing must be added to their education,
after the mantra training of summer vacation.

Rear View Mirror

My God, my God, why hast thou forsaken me?
—St. Matthew, Chapter 27, Verse 46

I really should not have been driving—
only my death grip on the wheel held me upright.
Glancing through tear-fogged glasses,

I saw that I had forgotten to give Eli his beloved book
of barnyard animals, gnawed and swollen with saliva;
I touched the soggy keepsake and exploded into sobs.

E'li, E'li, Ia' ma sa-bach' tha-ni.

Ten miles further south on Route 5,
calm enough to check the rearview mirror,
I found it filled with the snow-covered Mt. Shasta.

This vision followed me for forty miles.
The surveyors of the road from Sacramento
had drawn a straight line to the heart of the volcano.

Oh Shasta, giver and taker of life,
will you be his mother now?
Please?

After eleven years of autism, I am all out of miracles.
From the rearview mirror Shasta echoed,
All you had to do was ask...ask...ask.

Eli and Louise's Retardation

No one knew
we had anything to type
Because we didn't type anything

We were too busy being retarded

We have been guided
to separate homes
Where it's safe
to tell them
who we are
You with your communication board
Me with my poems

We were retarded because
I thought
I could lead
both of our lives.

Mom, Tonapah Was the Greatest Horse in the World, Wasn't He?

Tonapah came to live with us
when you turned four.
He was huge and wise,
our first horse,
who came to teach us
about being huge and wise.

Isn't that Tonapah
the horse people would say,
as we rode through town,
his feathered feet flying.

We were new, he was experienced.
You helped feed, muck
and tack him up,
standing on a box
to reach his huge head
and pick out his hooves,
big as dessert plates.

You were such a fine child,
trained to take the reins
of the dynasty we were building,
with Tonapah huge and wise
down at the barn.

When you were eleven
Tonapah got old and cantankerous,
was sent to the Mexican meat packers,
after he slammed your leg into a fence.

There was no room
for any more mistakes. . . .
You clipped a lock of Tonapah's mane
the day he was sent down.

At nineteen you question everything,
even Tonapah.
Now the family is scattered, the dreams crushed.
Only you and Tonapah were the greatest,
only you are left.

On Finally Becoming a Good Mother

We sit in the still library
holding your hand as you
spell out your first request, ever.
Please. . . make. . . me. . . an. . . appointment. . .
with. . . a. . . minister. . . of. . . God. . . .

On the phone I tell
the recommended minister that I
don't know what you want.
That you are fourteen.
That you can't talk.
That you communicate only
with an alphabet board
if I hold your hand.

We drive to the appointment, you
in your new pants and maroon sweater.
You choose to wear diapers,
just in case.

In her office, you rock hard
in the chair, eyes closed.
I call for courage out loud
and hold your hand poised above
the alphabet board.

The minister leans towards you.
Do you have a question?

You begin,
How. . . do. . . you. . . pray?

Beautiful Eyes

My son at thirty,
lived in a highly-thought of
group home
(regarded as humane)
was distinguished by his penchant
for collecting Grateful Dead t-shirts
from the staff and his parents.

A visitor, offering him his first chance
to use a facilitated kind of
communication, asked him
if he really liked
collecting the t-shirts.

My son's typed response was:
No,
but the staff likes them.

Asked what he would prefer to receive,
he typed, *An education.*

We asked if we could repeat his story.

He typed, *Yes,*
if you tell them I have beautiful eyes.

The Miracle of Eli and the Floating Stone

Looking through the little window
into your classroom,
I am amazed to see four special students
facing the chalkboard
while the standing teacher
is talking and writing words
on the board.
Words.
A model twelve-year-old special student,
you are perched on the edge of your chair
in your white turtleneck and black jeans,
eyes riveted on the board.

The teacher writes as he lectures.
Mt. Shasta is an old volcano
made of many layers of basalt and pumice....
The teacher hands you a basalt stone.
You pass it to the next special student,
infamous for throwing stones.
He passes it gently to the next.
The teacher asks you
to pick up a pumice stone,
and put it in a bowl of water.
You stand up,
pick up the stone,
place it in the water,
and poke it with your finger.
It floats.
The classroom cheers.
A miracle.
Three months ago

no one knew you had any more intelligence
than a loyal dog
or that stones could float.

Sultans of Discombobulation

Rolling in the streets
the handicapped are
chanting if they can.

Who, who.
Who shall inherit the earth?

Like Sultans with retinues,
of trusted attendants,
pushing wheeled thrones,
these peacekeepers,
heads held high with padded braces,
hobble and babble with poetic potential.

Who, who.
Who shall inherit the earth?

Here come the Sultans
of discombobulation
discomfort, confusion,
roiling in their wake.

What shall we should we think?
How shall we should we feel?

These Sultans so essential,
mucking up all our schemes
insulting to our able,
expedient and clean, who
goose step off to war.

In That Case

I was writing beside a creek
when a horse approached for a drink.

He looked friendly, so I asked,
what is it like to be a horse?

"Why should I tell you?" he answered politely,
water dripping from his muzzle.

I am writing a poem
and would like your point of view.

"In that case I will tell you.
Do you know
the story of the rattle snake
and the meadow lark?"

I'm afraid I don't.

"How about the praying mantis
who fell in love with the sun fish?"

Nooo...

"Surely you must know the story
of the tiny women of the grass
who can't eat the seeds of wild wheat."

I shook my head.

"In that case I can't explain anything to you,"
said the horse as he walked away.

The Secret Sorrow of Drooling Cats

Sung to "My Favorite Things" from The Sound of Music.

pinworms from ponies and Spanish armadas
doctrines from deserts and canons of scripture
bitter dark chocolate and autistic boys
going to the beach and losing the dog

when the gas leaks—
and the pond's dry—
and the frogs all die—
utopias lead to the guillotine
Oh for a horse with wings

flying fish in kitchens and restored religion
Silicon start-ups and Indigo Buntings
melting persimmons and psychotic men
ruining Christmas by speaking in tongues

then there's pink eye—
and there's TB—
that won't respond to drugs—
tidal bore racing toward Mont Saint Michel
Oh, for that horse, that horse with wings. . . !

Eli's Hyena

It has even followed us into the burger shop
on low-slung haunches,
and I'm trying to fend it off.

"Eli, if you want the Serenity prayer
touch the letter S.
For the Past Life prayer touch P."
Prayers aren't working.

He shouts and pounds his head
hard with his fist.
The hyena has gotten so brazen
since Eli turned eighteen—
stalking him relentlessly,
waiting for an opening.

They bring our burgers.
A shining boy, huge eyes, endless lashes,
watches our struggles.
Is he autistic?
I answer, Yes.
He says he's a facilitator
—I, too, use a letter board in my class

with a boy who can't talk. We discovered
he's really good at math.

He hands me a slip of paper and leaves.

I keep touching it,

T. J. Troutner, 829-2889.
Eli grabs the paper, crumples it.

I lunge to save that little slip of paper.
The hyena sees the opening, attacks.
Eli leaps up, all six-feet-three unfolds.

He shouts desperately, his fist a jack-hammer,
ketchup from the burger spreads through his hair
like blood.

Asylum

Most of the time
I half expect
to be killed
in treacherous terrain
while galloping—
ground under
steel shoes.
Then, horse and rider unite
in the wild rocking rhythm.
Asylum.

Once I found asylum
breastfeeding my youngest,
who lived, but failed to flourish.
His terrible crossed eyes
had killed
half my expectations.
Then, mother and child united
in the calm rocking rhythm.

There is no holiness
without terror.

Promises of the Wild

Conjuring on the wind, the Red-tailed Hawk
calls out the dead in extremis.
The raptor's keen
for the lifeless mothers, hovering
frantic over their newborns,
gashes the veil
between the quick and the dead
so the dead can pour
into paradise.

Sinking down in the tall grass, the bobcat
lowers soft belly to bedrock,
smooth, silent,
a divine descent
that shields the newborns,
fastens the orphans
to the earth.

These feral ones
braid stillness and chaos,
echoes of our time,
which will not save us
only make it possible
to live.

The Secret of Poetry

When I am lonely, I think of death.
When I am thinking of death, I am lonely.

I suppose you are secretly lonely,
thinking of death, thinking of love.

I'd like, please, to leave on your sill
just one cold flower whose beauty

would leave you inconsolable all day.
The secret of poetry is cruelty.

Recollection at Fourteen (A Boy's Turbulent Days)

Still mute at fourteen
he began to pray
so full of hope
but speech never materialized.

Abandoning prayer, he sat brooding
using the gift of silence
until he remembered, like Yeats
    his own grave heaped on grave,
    his own birth heaped on birth.

At sixteen he spellbinds,
claiming nine lives he spelled on the letter board,
describing how he
    saw Rome burn,
    made bricks in Africa,
    murdered his mother with strychnine,
    was betrayed by his wife
    on the shores of Lake Geneva.

Today, he and his mother pray
using Yeats' recollection of a deep talk
with Mohini Chatterjee of Bengal.

Prayer Before Sleeping
    I have lived many lives.
    I have been a slave,
    I have been a prince.
    Many a beloved has sat upon my knees.
    I have sat upon the knees of many a beloved.
    Everything that has ever been,
    shall be again. . . .

Part 3:
No Coin, No Ferry,
No Oars

About the Author at Fifty

I was writing a little biography
for a local publication—
Born and raised on the East Coast,
lived in California for the last 25 years,
three sons,
publishing history, blah, blah, blah,

suddenly it's Halloween
and friends are gathering
at our lesbian household.
At midnight
when the veil is thinnest
and sticky plates and cabernet bottles
are strewn everywhere,

Patience, a real Californian,
takes off her clothes in the spirit of comfort.
Horrified by her license,
I long to suck the whole party
into the Electrolux.

Patience laughing, says, *Oh Louise,*
are you going to ruin
a wonderful buzz by vacuuming?
At 1 A.M. I change my bio:
Louise Whitney was born
and raised on the East Coast,
fled to California, and 25 years later
became her mother.

Plate Tectonics

One volcano, Mt. Shasta,
breathing in deep meditation,
takes my son under her shadow,
and loves him.

Submerged in the Atlantic trench,
volcanic factories
exhale lava pillows,
paving stones for the expanding ocean floor.

Long ago, these pillows
pushed the Atlantic Ocean
over the Rock of Gibraltar,
filling up the Mediterranean Valley.

This same fluid flows in my veins.
How else could I know that a volcano
loves my son?

Small Snail Meditation

Scores of snails glide up
the meditating Buddha
and meet on his head
to protect him from the sun.

I meditate on my fish tank
and the vicissitudes of its balance,
constantly allusive
due to the fecundity of the snails.

I protect my aquatic sanctum
by reaching in daily,
God-like hand
culling three snails,
tossing them under the oak tree
beside the kitchen door.

This lapse in compassion
is the only path I know
to balance.

I cannot sit still
to suffer the snails
to do what they will.

No Coin, No Ferry, No Oars

It's raining and I sit by the fire
sinking in liquid thoughts,
sinking forty miles below my chair
down to the hot sea, the liquid magma.

This house is full of little hot spots:
four burners on the stove, four flames all lit
only when the whole family gathers;
the nightly fire in the living room,
a cord of walnut a year to draw the hot element to us.
Just enough heat to imagine
we have coin for the ferry.

It's clearing outside and I can see
stars above the Monterey cypress.
It's a mere forty miles to outer space
where the earth loses influence,
where I float, frigid, untethered by gravity,
without oars for the alien sea.

I recoil to the warm fire on the earth's skin
make that short trip again
sinking in slow motion
through the crust to the molten lava sea.
I will sit and wait for the old volcano,
Mount Diablo, to erupt.
Wait for the magma to consume my home,

explode the cypress,
mock my little hot spots.
There will be no coin, no ferry, no oars.

Under Oak

We started clandestine with summer mornings
surging up the mountain on sweating horses
to our oak grove, our first bedroom,
where the horses, stamping off flies, kept guard
as we strained to get our boots off,
oblivious to the sharp rocks and prickly foxtails
pressing into our bare backs.

We end years later under a mother oak,
our four-poster bed sinking
slowly into white lace-covered feathers.
This is the room where I've
slept and woken with you,
the horses safely in their stalls.

We are surprised now
when lust, like a flash flood,
takes over and washes us
clean of expectations.

Dominatrix

She would have made a good wife
had she not a secret passion for serpents,
a delight in murder,
a covert craving for the sweet piercing of thorns,
the need to spend three months of the year
with the sly—the barren—the damned.

She believed in ecstasy, refused to be damned
to a lifetime as some man's wife.
But she wanted health insurance as the years
passed, in case she was bitten by one of her serpents
or got infections from her many thorn
wounds. She didn't have a lawyer if caught in a murder

dragnet. More likely, she would be the murder
victim of one of the many lovers who damned
her to hell and wished her body thrown on the thorns
of the cacti surrounding her house. No good wife
could allow so many poisonous serpents
congregating, more each year

because she fed them. As cacti and the years
wrapped around her, and the sun murdered
her skin, she came to resemble the sly serpents
that lived under the front porch. That damned
rotten porch that almost made her wish she was a wife
and could chase out the snakes and hack back the thorns.

Truth is, she had a greater love for thorns
than comfort, and in the two thousandth year
of our Lord, she realized that Jesus never had a wife,

and his reward for teaching light and love was murder.
Jesus loved Mary Magdalene and never damned
her for her love of serpents.

So she resolved to suffer her beloved serpents
and proudly wear a crown of thorns
like Jesus who loved the damned
the most, and in her fiftieth year
renounced her elaborate plot to murder
an old lover who had abandoned her to be another man's wife.

Despite the serpents that multiplied with the years,
despite the thorns and murder
intrigues, she would have made Jesus a damned good wife.

The Blade that Spares None

She told her daughter stories
of mystical swordswomen,
The Black Butterfly, The Lady with the Sword,
The Blade that Spares None.

The daughter, listening at her feet
wondered how her mother
could ever be a swordswoman
with her feet partially deformed.

The ancestors had attempted foot binding
but the spirited child unraveled the bandages
again and again,
until it was too late to crush all the bones.

This child made certain that foot binding
would never be the fate of her daughter.
But her daughter's feet were deformed
by a French ballet mistress who insisted on toe shoes

because women were creatures of the air
and must appear immune to the laws of gravity.

Butterfly Garden

Cynthia Annabella, a West Coast Lady,
visits my Butterfly Bush every year.
Painted Ladies prefer Stinging Nettles,
Red Admirals always follow Painted Ladies.
I've planted a patch of Wild Buckwheat
for the Gray Hairstreak
but she'll only sip California Coffeeberry.
I've got Mallow for Swallowtails,
Lupin for Echo Blues,
Milkweed for Monarchs.
I thought Angel Wing would love Hollyhock,
but she has eyes only for Naughty Marietta.

Queen Elizabeth the First

My neighbor has chosen never to marry.
She has many suitors and is *très Nanook*
with her matching yellow kayaks—
her tiny armada.

She is a fan of Queen Elizabeth the First
and tells me the queen tranquilized her suitors
with tax revenues from sweet wine,
magic sweet wine.
When they displeased her
she cut off their heads.

My neighbor wears glasses and says that
if Elizabeth had been cursed with poor eyesight
her best hope would have been the King of Spain.

Fortunately her vision was perfect,
so today we see The Queen, her
royal robes falling over the flanks
of her white stallion,
her hooded falcon grasping
her gloved fist.

The Hotel Think About It

Kigali, Rwanda

I had a Tutsi friend long ago—
Wanyama, he was very tall.

All the Tutsi men are beautiful

too beautiful for work.
We leave that to short people, the Hutu.

A Tutsi man never works,
he practices jumping high.

The taller you are, the higher the jump.
That is our purpose,

to be higher than the Hutu.
He unfolded his languid body

into the African night
and shot three feet straight up.

What We Learned at the Blue Bird School

William Tell refused to take off his hat to the king.
Haile Selassie was a direct descendant of Solomon and Sheba.
Our teacher's nephew discovered the bird of paradise.
Arturo Toscanini was almost a god.

Haile Selassie was a direct descendant of Solomon and Sheba
but kings and queens are un-American.
Arturo Toscanini was almost a god
because he broadcast the symphony orchestra on the radio.

Kings and queens are un-American
but it's the Song of Solomon we remember.
Toscanini broadcast the symphony on the radio
to uplift Americans.

It's the songs we remember
because of the radio
which uplifts Americans
who do not have kings.

Because of the radio
we became America
which does not have kings.
We wore feathers of the bird of paradise.

We became America,
uplifted by our broadcasts,
wore feathers of paradise in our hats
until the birds were gone.

Oh My God It's Hector

Walking to the Golden Gate Bridge,
I behold four logging trucks, laden
with one giant Sequoia.
Four chariots, blue doors decorated
in white filigree, each pulled
by five hundred horses, thunder past me
and past me and past me spewing
diesel fumes and bits of bark.

Through the city the chariots
drag Hector, fallen,
cut down by triumphant Achilles,
cut and cut and cut and cut
in leviathan sections, distributed
over the four-truck caravan.

The street fills with business as usual
as this profane rite of triumph
passes by the Golden Gate of Troy.

Mellifluous

Leta the hand therapist leads
me to a tank of warm wax.

Nine times, she lowers my frozen hand
into the honey clear liquid

but it's her voice....

I close my eyes, remember
the Queen of Thailand

when she came to California to receive an award.
Her retainers roll

a purple carpet down the aisle
for her march to a gilded throne.

Beside the podium, her lady in waiting
kneels, offering the queen's glasses

on a brocade pillow. Placing them
on her face, she begins

in a voice, so mellifluous
it stuns her audience.

This is the sound of a real queen,
liquid and warm
like honey.

Rondonia, Brazil

The burning jungle is background
for a lone water skier, caiman jigger,
broken diving board, waiting
for the man who never came up.

A hunted Nazi sells
mahogany toilet seats
with his snow-blue eyes.

Bottle in one hand,
the mayor of a new town
publicly sodomizes a boy
while swearing himself in.

Indians step shyly from the jungle
onto the red road scar
like blinking fawns.

Inoculation guns at the bus terminal
shoot the desperate arrivals
before they stream into the jungle
to burn it down.

The dying monkey claws at the arrow
imbedded in her side,
crushes it with pointed teeth

I want this arrow as a souvenir.

The Indian guide won't give it to me,
says it isn't good any more.

Thunder Road Home

A fat joint and the doctor is
behind the wheel
of her new Mazda RX-7,
arms stretched to the steering wheel
flying the road
from San Francisco,
home to the high desert.

I love her especially
when she drives
the mountain passes.
Part mule
part California condor.

An old girl on
a yellow and black Harley
tips her helmet
as she roars past,
posture perfect,
rubber face flapping,
eager to get to the big
Harley biker swarm up in Reno.

A long smooth toke
and a long smooth left.
We feel the difference
between going left and going wrong.
Up and over
to her family
in the high desert.

We borrow her sister's
four-wheel-drive truck,
the dashboard littered
with dust-caked open bills,
crushed Marlboro packs,
an eyelash curler,
melted Maybelline mascara.

She lives near the wild
Mustang holding pens
on the long road
through Paiute country
to Pyramid Lake.

The doctor takes me to a coyote
cave high in the Pyramids,
where her father taught
her to climb as if
there were a rattler
on every rock.

Bones of rodents litter
the cave floor,
but the cave is filled
with the spirits
of lake fish, lurking.

Muse of the Seraglio

When the moon is full of jasmine

Glide beneath the padlocked door and
slide slowly down my spine

Penetrate the secret grief
that never seems to find release.

Teach me, the velvet dance
the polished flick of forked tongue

The kiss that so impressed Eve
she gave away the garden.

Mark me, in some secret place
then strum
no
drum me

I beg you,
lift your shuddering hips

and call my name.

Hildegard von Bingen at The Blue Mermaid Motel

She wanted nothing tawdry to spoil this rendezvous
so she chose "The Blue Mermaid" from the yellow pages
just for its appealing name.

For luscious hours, she searched her music collection
for the perfect mood of absolution
finally choosing the ancient hymns of the Abbess

Hildegard von Bingen, advisor to saints and popes.
She drove to three flower shops to gather enough freesia
to mask the odor of stale motel smoke.

Placing a bouquet on the bedside table
she slipped Hildegard into the boom box,
the tape prearranged to orchestrate their need.

O *ignis spiritus* poured over their trembling bodies
for five minutes and eleven seconds.
followed by *Ave generosa*...

(Thank you, thank you ambrosial Abbess)
And the finale, nine minutes and fifty-seven seconds of
        O *Jerusalem*....

Narrowing the Possibilities of Life Between Us

On the way to my new hairdresser
I compose an ecstatic poem
about truth telling
between lesbian women,
the lies of the patriarchy
and terror of the dark core.

The hairdresser is darkly handsome,
from India via Fiji and London.
Draped and disoriented,
I hear myself say
that I have a part interest
in a tropical flower farm in Hawaii—
which certainly isn't true.

Forkéd Tongue Incantation

You've gone, whose duty was to please,
to penetrate the secret grief
that never here could find relief.

I'll bring you back
by force of will,
with my own hand
extract my heart,
fan the fire
with my art.

Another now lies
next to you.
You may rule her
with a kiss, discipline
through tenderness.

Like the serpent
I will glide
underneath the bedroom door.
But my tongue
on your dark eyes,
will be colder than the moon.

For I prefer to terrorize.

Part 4:
Woodstock

A Valentine

(Mostly stolen from E.E. Cummings)

Eli, I have never travelled gladly
beyond any experience, but
your eyes have a silence.

Nothing we perceive in this world
equals the texture
of your stories,
rendering death and forever
with each silent telling.

I do not know what it is
that closes and opens, but
something understands
the voice of your eyes.

Not even the spring
has such ancient hands.

Slow Lava

The husband heard nothing
but the roaring of his own career.
Deaf to the rumbling in the magma
of his marriage, he left on business.

As his taxi drove away,
the wife, almost erupting in anticipation
of the unknown, called the fascinating woman.
You can come over now,
he is finally gone.

Shaking, they lay down on the bed.
The fascinating woman inched over hours
across forbidden territory toward
the wife feigning sleep, waiting
for the woman moving, moving like slow lava.

It Hurts to be Alive

You can't word your way out of someone else's pain.
You can make yourself less dangerous
with words. So far your

children are the hardest to convince. Beloved son,
a man now—has lost the future—his lover a lovely woman out
of a Jane Austen novel.

He thinks, maybe the hot part of the drama
is not enough
but that's the part he's perfected.

He's not completely lost:
he has his teaching,
his body, his screenplay, to hold him.

His old lesbian mother says,
Share your charm, charm your share
while you're still beautiful.

Meanwhile, she'd fly three thousand miles this minute
to pull the blankets up around his broad shoulders
as he lies sleeping.

What the Thunder Said

When birds lose their way to the sky,
and dogs sleep fitfully at our feet,

we need elephants, the thunder of a herd,
a cataclysm stampeding through the forest
trembling of earth and rocks
crack and crash of upturned trees.

The whole sky swells with their trumpeting
while man's best friend can only whine

to be taken for a walk.

A dog's company is no longer enough.

We need a greater friendship,
on the scale of our loneliness.

Belladonna

I'm compelled to court her,
touch her slowly, gently,
whisper
Belladonna

until suddenly
her displeasure flashes. With a heave
of her great head and neck

she throws her dark mane back,
dangerous,
perhaps lethal.

Abandoned by the desperate,
the mare appeared in the night,
melted into the herd.

"Whose horse is this, anyway?"
asks the ranch manager.

I want her.
Want to attend her.
She has kind eyes.

She will transform.
She will become
Belladonna, Belladonna.

I will use magic.

Log Book

From within a burning almond log,
a blowtorch, a Roman candle, spews
a stream of sparks from the fireplace.

Tame almond, carefully husbanded,
cut down for firewood when old.
Fiery burst of memory, stored, concealed,
waiting for this moment of revelation.

Are we witnessing an old happiness
in its limbs,
memory of a phoebe's nest,
the return each spring,
or a hawk gorging, a ground squirrel
grasped in one successful claw?

Or is it an old wound
from a careless pruning,
where deep frost entered, healed over,
and years later is released by fire,
which licks the old hurt until it bursts
onto our hearthstones?
The body forgets nothing.

Moon Mood

We're out here in the winter night
blowing smoke at the moon,
worshipping her face of many faces.

Tonight's questions are—

If freezing to death in the snow with your lover:

Do you search in vain for wood until you die
with the ax handle in your frozen hand?

Do you sacrifice yourselves in a suicide seduction pact
by throwing the ax handle into the fire
just to make the moon mood linger?

Music

There were no miracles,
only resentments
when friends suggested
     dolphin swimming
     vitamins
     special schools in far-off cities

Without speech,
I imagined goldfish thoughts
and kept hugging and kissing you,
thankful you didn't have wet scales.

Now Mount Shasta has
activated my dead volcano mind
with one typed word.

I didn't even know you knew letters
(you who sat with your back
to Sesame Street, listening).

When asked, *What do you want?*
with teacher's help you type,
M-U-S-I-C.

Eli, Eli,
I have so many questions to ask you.
Did I abandon you?
No, I'll not burden you
any more with my guilt,
I'll simply sing for you.

Nitrous Oxide

With a pick my Punjabi hygienist
escapes her village by the skin
of my teeth as she plows my numb roots.

A snood snug on my nose inspires
me to wax on between bee-stung gums
about the great Irish poet Seamus Heaney.

Who when young, was sent to stay alone
with a terrifying grandmother,
the one with the ghastly long fingernail.

He wept and wailed and the farm mother
did not say, "Child, what's the matter?"
She said, "Child, what *ails* you?"

That magical word, so exotic,
so unexpected, it, in his alarm,
led him from farm to library

until he recalled the check marks
of his teachers in County Derry
as "little leaning hoes."

Sargasso Sea

Two million square miles of seaweed floats on the surface of
the North Atlantic, east of the West Indies.

It's a hoodoo place,
with a ragged gold and olive roof
riddled with silver eels.
Between seedless clumps of weeds
long rays of sunlight penetrate
the deep—never reach bottom
where ghost ships,
once lacking luck, wind or current,
huddle in a silent rolling mass,
skeletons of ancient galleons,
slave ships, pirate ships, clipper ships.
When you avowedly hunt for trouble,
you find it.
Long John in silver earrings
clinging to the schooner's bowsprit,
fishing for the hoodoo fish
of the deep sea sailor—
the golden dolphin
which uncaught
brings luck and fair winds.

Following the Place at the Tip of My Tongue

I twist around in the big western saddle
cinched tight under the belly of my mare.
Hand shading my eyes, I follow

the flight of a golden eagle
as it rides the thermals in warm loops.
The eagle drops something—something

valuable, seminal, backlit by the sun.
A feather, a name, an idea
drifting across the yellow hills.

I spur the horse in pursuit
of whatever still calls to me,
a phrase I almost know,

shining on the wind.
We dash toward the Pacific,
then east, closing in on the falling prize.

The sweating horse, my soaring need,
follow the place at the tip of my tongue
where the dream I've forgotten hovers,

floats to ground
disappears, lost
in a sargasso

of poison oak, home
of slithering eel dreams
that once fell from heaven.

Armor

So weary after this day of horror
assembling his psychiatrist and the police,
she finally dares to take off her armor,
piece by piece.
Off with the big black bra
its heavy underwire forcing, molding
those breasts which once suckled him.
Off with the war paint, the mask,
eyeliner, mascara, lipstick.
Off with the polished silver earrings.
Off with her big amber ring
with the mosquito trapped
forty million years ago:
one fragile wing open,
the other, crushed.

And to My Granddaughter, Emily Hope Whitney, I Leave My Diamond

I inherited from my mother
and she from hers
the hardest thing on earth.

A diamond, an elemental stone
full of crystallized courage,
memorized starlight.

Only words have the power
to turn stones into jewels,
treasures

so precious
they bring memory
to life.

This diamond,
atomic number 6,
radiates

on my ring finger
turns mythic
on three words

       mother
       grandmother
       touchstone

Thoroughbred

And now I have enough
to tame me, to break
me and might be expected
to stand still in my stall,
but I do not.
Headlong
I was in the beginning
and headlong I continue,
my Italian tattooed inside my upper lip.
Testa Lunga
galloping through tangles,
the bit in my teeth.
Testa Lunga guessing
at the meaning of words,
expecting each moment to be
erased by the next,
and thunder
to be quick as lightning.

Chantress of Amon

1070-945 B.C.

I sit alone with the body of the Chantress,
trying to imagine what she sang,
while she lies shriveled in her coffin,
her arms crossed over her chest,
prepared for eternity... *Don't worry,*

the Chantress won't be on the final,
says the young professor to her class.
To me she says, *So sorry...*
as they noisily arrange their portable stools
in a semicircle around me and the body

cut three thousand years ago with stone ritual knives
to remove her brain and viscera.
Two students have already gone to sleep.
Their heads hang on their chests. *The Egyptians
of the twenty-first dynasty,* explains the professor,

*filled her cavities with sweet-smelling myrrh
and spices, submerged her in a salt solution,
dried and swathed her in strips of linen.
Funerary scenes from "The Book of the Dead"
surround her coffin. Notice the Eye of Horus.*

A student with an English accent, pink-cheeked,
asks about the significance of eyes
in ancient Egyptian art. *Sorry,
eyes are not my speciality.*
She points to a canopic jar of alabaster

topped by gods: human-headed Amsat

guards the Chantress' liver,
jackal-headed Dua-mulef, her stomach,
falcon-headed Kabeh-senu-ef, her intestines.
Two more students nod off.

And I, who was in a romantic rhapsody,
alone with the long-dead Chantress
inhaling her breath, her song,
now start calculating the money
this class is costing the parents

as the professor stretches up on her toes,
trying to reach her sleepy students,
while baboon-headed Hapi guards the lungs
of the Chantress of Amon, who once
sang the sun up, and woke the dreamers.

Conference of the Mute
Sacramento Hilton, January, 2001

Tomorrow I will be my absolute best
at the gathering of the voiceless, the mute.

Desperation is the price of admission to the
place of dissipated dreams and paralyzing stigmas,
place where *talk* can hardly be tested
and reality *checks* don't hold up in court.

No more miracle cures
just a minimum of lies
and terrible, hard, work

Believe: A voice can be found for anyone.
Don't Believe: and get left out of the mystery.

The best way to prepare
is with poetry, adult diapers and a plastic sheet.

I was born for this.

Optimism of Crows

Two black satin ladies perch on the bed
rustling like crows, wings low overhead.
The death watch is over. They've buried their dead.

They preen their black feathers preparing for sleep,
take off their earrings, then both of them reach
for the cold cream, to smooth their crow's feet.

Address Book

On the front flap
for easy access
an unstable list of 5 phone numbers
of fellow seekers
who support me
day or night
on the path
to serenity

On the back flap
for easy access
an unstable list of 5 stocks
and the number of my stockbroker
who supports me
during office hours
in buying time
to write poetry

In between the flaps
in alphabetical order
The rest of my life

The State

Four polywogs and six newborn guppies later
King Bhumibol, the Siamese Fighting Fish,
was finally full

He had waited craftily
in the plants placed by the State especially
to protect the babies

The peasant guppy had labored amongst the plants.
King Bhumibol snatched her babies
as they parted from her body

She seemed unconcerned
even interested in a snack herself

So the State, considering itself benevolent,
considered studying up on Darwin
and letting the king manage the tank
or planting more plants.

The Silence of Knives

On Easter Sunday
I lost my favorite knife
the one for cutting
avocados, cheese and bread

Knife, oh knife, I called
Come cut me free
from this burden of ceremony

From the depths
of the kitchen drawer
came only silence

Woodstock

Friday, driving up the New York thruway
with the Greek ambassador in the back seat of the Ferrari,
we worried that the heavy traffic of hippies
was also going to the races at Saratoga.
When the butler greeted us with champagne,
we forgot the inconvenience.

Saturday, a friend's filly was running.
We watched her come in second from our box.

Sunday, dressed in immaculate white,
torrential rain drove us from the grass court
to settle inside to drink more champagne.

Monday, we took a spin in the antique yacht
moored on Lake Champlain.

Tuesday, driving back to the city,
there was such an unaccountable crush of hippies
we were forced to turn on the radio
and hear that we missed Woodstock,
the cultural event of our generation.

Part 5:
The African Queen's
Tea Party

Canada Goose

You pick me up after my first boy-girl party.
We drive two and a half hours in the night
to the salt marsh on the Atlantic flyway.
You have decided that I am old enough.
Just you and me and my party dress.
Mum found the dress at Hutzler's.
Made me wear it.
Told me I'd have fun at the party.
She did help me pack a canvas bag,
clothes suitable for duck shooting: thick socks

rubber boots
heavy sweater
jacket.
You stop the car on the dirt road
miles into the marsh.
You want me to hear something.
We get out.
I shiver in my dress and little high heels
furious at my wrongness,
for you are never cold.

Listen—
It's a party of thousands
mostly couples
mated for life
chatting intimately.
More beings talking together
than at the ball game.
More than when we are all together

in study hall.
They have come here for the winter.
They fly to Canada for the summer.
We go to Maine for summer.
Baltimore for winter.
How do you know these invisible
chatty beings in the night marsh?
They are polite and don't stop
talking because we have arrived.
My father and I are welcome
at their party
in the winter night marsh
in my party dress.

Summer Reading in the Hamptons

Their private library was round
and soared three mahogany floors
through the middle of the house.
The babysitter, who knew a few things,
chose a different book every two days,
to take to the beach.

She knew the first printed book,
the Gutenberg Bible, was key in spreading the Word,
as she spread *The Great Gatsby* on the sand,
cracked its spine, kept the pages
from fluttering in the sea breeze
with a sweating Coca Cola bottle.

She knew the printing press was vital
in calling out summer soldiers
to the American Revolution,
as she marked passages of *Lady Chatterley's Lover*
with folded corners
for an intimate read in the tender night.

She did not know
that all those sandy, dog-eared,
broken-backed, coke-ringed books
were first editions.

Learning to Listen

My father was a secret agent in Siam.

Searching for clues to my destiny,
I travelled to his mythological land
to meditate on the backs of elephants,
in temples, and tiger-teeming jungles.
Each time I received the same clear directive,
Get Guppies.
No, no, no, I want a real message,
and tried again in a candle-lit cave
filled with chanting monks.
Again the directive,
Get Guppies.

Home in California, feeling no wiser
for all my exotic travel,
I drove to the Sea Horse Aquarium,
purchased a ten-gallon tank, sand, plants,
and four guppies: two males and two females.
I added water, put them on the kitchen table,
and watched
as a universe unfolded over time,
changing the way I listen.

Arsenic is Made With Peach Pits

She doesn't even have to lift her head
off her parents' pillows to watch
the sun rise over the Atlantic,
bringing the 6 A.M. lobster boat
chugging under her window
with its amusing cloud of laughing gulls
and static of its ship-to-shore radio.

Whiskey Tango 6802, come in, come in,
over the whine of the vacuum cleaner two floors below.
This lesbian daughter lies in her bed guilty as charged
dreading, dreading
the parental breakfast of fresh coffee and blueberry muffins
in this historic old house, full of family
and impossible expectations, governed
by a perfect August morning.

Preparing her Orgasmic Memory

She sears sensation into her psyche.
Each orgasm a consummate journey
of ecstasy and death, like plum blossoms,
nearly forgotten until the next epiphany.

She will have better luck remembering
consummate journeys riding emotional horses.
Journeys she's now burning into her bones,
which will grow light with age.

Winter in Hamlin

It is winter, she is cold, deflated
like an old woman's handbag, stained

a desiccated calfskin that no amount
of leather balm can ever resurrect.

Gone is the nourishing music of clouds
cirrus, cumulonimbus of summer.

Now there are only sleek rats gorging
on her meager rations in the root cellar.

Gone is the eerie spell of the bagpipe
inflated goatskin rhythmically squeezed

between ribs and elbow, forcing clouds
of spectral weather through a punctured pipe

while some nimble-fingered lover
moved her hands as if she had a plan

as if there was more than a low-pitched drone
as if the rats would follow the piper.

The Woman Who Fed Animals

*It is always better to avenge dear ones than to indulge
in mourning.* —Seamus Heaney's "Beowulf"

In the glory land of honor
there lived a woman who was not beautiful
and did not inspire legends in the great halls.

All her life she fed animals.
From sun up to down she prepared and carried food
to animals and people. It was all the same to her.

The years passed. Her back became bent,
her eyesight weak. Still she kept providing,
resting only at dark when she listened

for the howling of wolves.
One night when the moon was full
the howling near and fierce,

old and weary, she hobbled from her warm
hearth fire to check the chickens.
The wolves waiting, hungry,

tore off her bowed legs, her gnarled hands,
fed on the woman who fed animals
in the glory land of honor.

Digging to China

Children at the beach probe the crust
with their hands. Using trust as a tool
to pierce mantle and magma, their arms
stretch down hopeful holes to touch
the fingers of Chinese children.
At arms' length they abandon the quest,
ingest the crust in sandy sandwiches.
Satisfied, they swim.

Years pass. The trust tool shrinks.
Their arms lengthen into diamond drills,
screw bore holes in the crust.
The deepest is too shallow,
and they can't stand sandy sandwiches.
Dissatisfied, they use sound waves,
probe mantle and magma, seldom swim.

An American Story

Uncle Edward's great grandmother died
just short of her hundredth birthday.
When she was a little girl
she knew George Washington.

Uncle Edward died
just short of *his* hundredth birthday.
When he was a little boy, *he* knew *her*.

So Uncle Edward knew someone
who knew George Washington.

When I told this story to a Persian friend,
he exclaimed, "My God,
that would be just like knowing
someone who knew Cyrus the Great!"

Labyrinth

Do not step on the emaciated rat
gagging in the maze of artichokes,
or on the three-eyed child
huddled by the oven
drying the sweaty socks of Jesús.

Do heed this warning—
that labyrinth
contains chemicals
known to the State of California
to cause cancer,
or reproductive harm.

Don't ask the Minotaur,
beast of the endless rows,
if he knows a path to the Pacific.

He will tell you it is too far,
too dark, too late.

Horse Power

The car cops and the horse cops sit bantering
in the heat outside the Reno, Nevada courthouse—
bantering about horse power.

The taciturn horse cops catch the brunt of it
while their gleaming steeds stamp off flies
at the hitching post

right next to the line of shiny cop cars.
It's time for the afternoon shift.
They drop their styrofoam cups in the trash,

saunter towards their various transports.
The horse cops in tall black boots
pull on long gauntlet gloves.

One bends over, picks up a tidy ball of manure
with his gloved hand, launches it casually
skyward over his shoulder, over two cars

where it arcs through the opening door of a third,
falls perfectly onto the floor
beneath the steering wheel.

The African Queen's Tea Party

When I was twenty-one and unmarried,
I stepped around ten agéd Queens
of the dead King, sitting on the floor
in the dim light guarding,
with the rest of their lives,
his fingernail cuttings, stuffed leopard,
shields, spears and umbilical cord.

I stepped through their thatched world of obligation,
out the guarded exit into the courtyard,
where light pierced my eyes
and walked into the well-lit palace
of the modern reigning Queen and only wife
of the mighty King of the Baganda.

The Queen approached down a long hall
in a cotton dress, bare feet on polished tile.
All in her court, except me,
prostrated themselves full length
and stayed there, heads down,
while she clapped twice for tea
and patted a chair next to her throne.

"Where are you from Louise?"
"I am from Baltimore,
45 minutes north of Washington D.C."
"Baltimore! Do you know the town of
Timonium?"
"Yes, it is only five minutes from my home."

"Do you know the Head ski factory there?"

the Queen queried.
"Yes, I visit frequently."
"So do I, to pick a good pair
for skiing in San Moritz."

We chatted about skiing
until the queen made her exit.
The court got off their faces.
I left the palace, walked out to the courtyard
then back through the dim crone hall,
stepping around the ten former queens

in 1964, when I was twenty-one and unmarried.

Receiving the Fiftieth Rejection Slip
After a Run of Beginner's Luck

I need a fish, a fix, a fancy fin.
I've watched the others reel them in,
even hooked a few myself.

I caught a bass, a perch, a walleye pike;
found the backwater fish would bite
ironic worms from my manure pile.

Went to school to learn a new technique;
hand-tied my flies and cast them deep
into the post-modern pool.

I caught a block, a rash, an attitude.
It wasn't long till l was imbued
with self-pity and despair.

I need a fish, a fix, a fancy fin.

Wet Welded Together

There is a woman in a rage riding the rain.
Riding low on the neck of her mare
they surge up Black Mountain.

The mare born to run up mountains,
one half thoroughbred for speed,
one half Arab for endurance.

The woman born to rage,
one half mother of sons
one half lover of women.

The woman's rage is the mare's joy.
The mare's joy becomes the woman's,
as they race, wet welded together.

Beach Shoes

I have come to love
even your beach shoes
and take care to knock

all the sand out of both.
Each grain a miracle
which might cause torment.

From my well-watered edge,
I used to think
all this tenderness

was the fault, yes fault,
of a finicky beginning
encased in shoes.

Now I know
the vex of your high desert.
How its heart-stop rattle

of constant snakes,
its wicked cactus spines,
forbade bare feet.

I am here
to protect
your tenderness.

Dust Ruffle

I've reefed the mainsail
of my middle-aged ship,
which has sprung some leaks.
The occasional horse,
being lowered into my hold,
is dropped onto the deck.
A beloved offspring
occasionally falls overboard.
All this can be caulked,
splinted, medicated.
There is still time to release the reef.

My parents have furled
the sails of their aged ship,
now moored upriver,
silver, stairs and jewels
jettisoned to stay afloat.
No hold at all to lower horses into.
But the bright work, the bright work
is immaculate.
Below the deck, in their stateroom,
a dust ruffle billows
around their double berth, or death.

Colophon

This book uses for body type *Sabon*.
Jan Tschichold (1902-1974)
created *Sabon* in the early 1960s,
naming it after a Lyonnaise punchcutter who originally brought
the *Garamond* typeface to Frankfurt.
Mr. Tschichold was Penguin paperback's chief designer;
he was the initial developer of a clean, fresh and modern style
much revered by booklovers everywhere.

About Many Names Press
831-427-8805 khitt@manynamespress.com
P. O. Box 1038 Capitola, CA 95010

In 1993 Kate Hitt founded Many Names Press to exercise the
right to free speech and to give writers, poets and artists access
to free expression with offset job printing. In 1996, she began to
produce digital editions, trade editions, fine press and letterpress
books, chapbooks and broadsides, with special emphasis on fine
art reproduction, photography, feminism, diversity, the arts, civil
rights, nature, the environment, transpersonal psychology and
world affairs.

Appreciation is given to Robin Atwood for her insightful editing
of Louise's accomplished poems.

Chandler & Price Pilot Letter Press (built circa 1880)
Still In Use at Many Names Press